The Draw-A-Person

Catalogue for Interpretative Analysis

By

William H. Urban, M.A.

Published by
WESTERN PSYCHOLOGICAL SERVICES
WPS® 12031 Wilshire Boulevard
Los Angeles, CA 90025-1251
Publishers and Distributors

Western Psychological Services, Los Angeles, CA 90025

Copyright © 1963 by Western Psychological Services

All rights reserved.

Fifteenth printing: February 2006

Printed in the United States of America

9 8

ISBN: 978-087424-044-3

Not to be reproduced, adapted, and/or translated
in whole or in part without prior written permission
of Western Psychological Services.

www.wpspublish.com

TABLE OF CONTENTS

	Page Number
Introduction	1
Historical Background	1
DAP Administration	1
Interpretation of the DAP	3
Final Report	4
A Few Words of Caution	4
The Draw-A-Person Catalogue	7

Introduction

This catalogue is designed as a clinical aid for the interpretation of the DRAW-A-PERSON PROJECTIVE TECHNIQUE (DAP). As such it provides the clinician, practitioner, and student with various classificatory categories and the suggested interpretative hypotheses developed by specialists in the DAP. It is a compilation of important materials organized for ready and practical use in the interpretation of the DAP.

Much of the catalogue material is derived from the works of Bender, Buck, Goodenough, Hammer, Jolles, Machover, and other specialists in the field of projective drawings. The alphabetic arrangement was suggested by Jolles' **A Catalogue for the Qualitative Interpretation of the H-T-P.** Jolles' **Catalogue** and Machover's **Personality Projection in the Drawing of the Human Figure** provide most of the catalogue content.

Selection, elaboration, organization, and presentation of all materials are the author's sole responsibility.

Historical Background

Acute observers always have been able to detect emotional connotations in artwork. That various clinicians have been interested in classifying and validating intuitive hunches about the personalities of artists is not surprising. As early as 1885 Ebenezer Cooke noted that the drawings of young children reveal personality characteristics of the child. Between 1900 and 1915, two international research projects were initiated to investigate children's drawings. They collected material from cooperative teachers and clinicians in many countries. Unfortunately, however, these two studies never were completed although some preliminary findings were reported.

In the 1920s Florence L. Goodenough[1] wrote her **Measurement of Intelligence by Drawings**. She showed how drawings mirrored the intellectual development of the child and developed a scale for scoring drawings for mental age. Goodenough foresaw further development and use of drawings to study personality: her insight has proved quite sound.

The works of Bender, Buck, Hammer, Jolles, Levy, Machover, and others have expanded the knowledge of projective drawings. Much of their work is summarized in concise form and reduced to interpretative hypotheses in this catalogue. Such materials can be used by those with a background in dynamic personality theories to delve into a subject's inner recesses, i.e., the denied, nonacceptable, repressed impulses.

DAP Administration

The administration of the DAP is deceptively simple. All that is required is a stack of 8½" x 11" white paper and a well-sharpened No. 2 black lead pencil. These are placed within easy reach of the subject so he may select a sheet of paper, place it, and use it as he desires.

He is told: "PLEASE DRAW A PICTURE OF A PERSON."

No further instructions need be given, as the purpose is to provide the subject with as nearly an unstructured situation as is possible. Questions raised by the subject are answered:

"THAT IS UP TO YOU. YOU MAY DO AS YOU LIKE."

The DAP is based on the assumption that an individual will be forced to structure this relatively unstructured situation in accordance with his basic, typical,

---

[1]Goodenough, Florence L., **Measurement of Intelligence by Drawings**, Yonkers-on-Hudson, New York: World Book Company, pp. 1, 78-80.

and unique personality dynamics, revealing essential data about himself through his approach to the task of drawing a person. It also is assumed that in his drawing of a person he will present, to some degree, both his self-image and his ideal self-image. He may, of course, present a person of significance to him: parent, sibling, spouse, teacher, etc.

During the examination, the Examiner closely observes the behavior of the subject, recording the spontaneous verbalizations. The entire behavior complex unfolded during the testing situation needs to be studied, evaluated, and interpreted. This awareness of the totality of the personality within the DAP testing milieu is of prime consideration during the interpretation of the DAP test results.

During DAP testing the subject may be concerned about the artistic qualities of his drawings. It is permissible to assure the subject that this is not a test of artistic ability and that artistic ability, as such, is not really considered when the test is scored and interpreted. It seems best to explain to the curious subject that DAP drawings are helpful in understanding the thinking and feeling of the subject.

It is ESSENTIAL to impart to the subject the importance of the DAP, its confidential nature, and its place as a routine procedure. Otherwise subjects may be unduly resistive to the test, either drawing stick figures or stylized drawings or possibly refusing the testing **in toto**.

When the first figure is drawn, the Examiner asks the subject to draw a figure of the opposite sex. The Examiner is careful to avoid using the words "male" or "female" permitting the subject to define his first figure as male or female. Occasionally a subject claims that his first figure is nonsexual. It is permissible for the subject to draw another figure and continue with a drawing of the opposite sex, or else he can consider the first figure as of either sex, whichever he desires.

If the subject's drawings are stereotyped figures, i.e., stick figures, cartoons, or stylized drawings, it is fruitful to repeat the test until a complete figure is drawn. Upon completion of the DAP, the Examiner thanks the subject for his cooperation and marks the drawings to indicate the name of the subject, his age, sex, date of testing, and sequence of drawings.

There are interesting variations of the DAP. For example, it is sometimes useful to use two sheets of paper with a carbon sheet between so a duplicate of the original drawing is made. The duplicate sheet clearly reveals erasures and permits the Examiner the opportunity of asking the subject if he would care to make changes in his original drawing: changes made, of course, can be compared with the carbon of the original drawing. Such changes indicate areas of concern and/or difficulty. "Normal" individuals tend to make changes which improve figures, showing better balance and control; anxiety-ridden persons tend to make changes which reveal poor control, rigidity, brittleness, and constriction.

Rigid and evasive subjects typically seek to avoid revealing themselves and attempt to devalue the testing situation by drawing stick figures or minimal representations of people. With these subjects, it is productive to request a drawing of a complete figure. This is somewhat equivalent to "testing the limits" in **Rorschach** test administration.

One objective in DAP testing is to stimulate subjects to produce more materials so evasiveness is spread thin and does not cover all defects. Subjects are "pushed" slightly to determine if they continue being rigid, guarded, constricted, or are able to expose resources.

It is valuable to request subjects to draw detailed heads or busts if they have drawn figures which lack head details. The head area is the most reliable indicator of the self-concept and the ability to deal with the social environment. In DAP theory, the head is the locus of the sense of self.

Other DAP variations include:
1. **Draw-A-Person-In-The-Rain**
2. **Draw-An-Animal**
3. **Draw-A-Member-Of-A-Minority-Group**

However, these variations are time-consuming and add little to the standard DAP.

Interpretation of the DAP

Interpreting the DAP appears deceptively simple and superficial to some; to others, it seems to be an extremely difficult and incomprehensible task.

An initial step in DAP interpretation is merely to describe the figures drawn. Are they young or old? Active or inactive? Flexible or rigid? Handsome or ugly? Massive or diminutive? Happy or sad? Formal or casual? Muscular or weak and atrophied? Aggressive and dominant or passive? Many such questions can be raised and can suggest various interpretative hypotheses concerning the subject who has drawn such figures. The assumption here is that perception of body image through drawings involves projections of personal feelings which unconsciously guide subjects in dealing with the DAP examination.

Some Examiners ask the subjects themselves to describe the figures they have drawn, using phrases such as:

"COULD YOU TELL ME WHAT SORT OF PERSON THIS DRAWING REMINDS YOU OF?"

"WHAT SORT OF A PERSON IS HE (OR SHE)?"

"MAKE UP A LITTLE STORY ABOUT THIS PERSON."

The more naive subject often will reveal important data concerning himself during such a procedure, thereby increasing the clinical validity of the DAP.

Although the above procedures may not be standardized DAP techniques of interpretation, they provide useful beginnings from which the Examiner can derive more meaningful hypotheses. In addition, they enable the Examiner to compare his descriptions with those of his co-workers and of the subjects, too.

Following this initial phase of description, the Examiner should study four major areas of the DAP drawings:
1. **Head**
2. **Hands, Arms, Shoulders and Chest**
3. **Torso**
4. **Legs and Feet**

The goal here is to identify the areas of **conflict, exaggeration, omission,** and **distortion**. Which body parts receive special emphasis through shading, size, or denial by being omitted? Where has the subject erased? Which lines are emphasized? Which lines are dim? Where does motor control break down? Where are there wavy lines and breaks in the lines? Once these areas of unusual treatment have been found, the interpretative hypotheses in this Catalogue can be listed. Such a simple listing later will be examined for inconsistencies and used for further analyses.

Consider the above mentioned four major areas:

First there is the head. It is the locus of the sense of self or the ego. It deals perceptively with the outer world. The eyes and the ears receive stimuli or extrapersonal data. The brain organizes and interprets this data and provides integration and intellectual control over the response systems. The mouth serves as an inlet for taking things into the body, i.e., (oral dependency) and as an outlet for aggression, friendliness, and other feelings. In the area of the head, intellectual aspirations and frustrations manifest themselves. Here also love is accepted, rejected, or ignored. So, too, the world of other human beings is accepted, rejected, or dealt with in some manner. Glamour aspirations may reveal themselves in the facial detailing. Contempt, hatred, and deep aggression may be seen in dark, piercing eyes. Oversensitivity and even suspiciousness may be seen in unusual ear detailing. The head can provide the Examiner with the most valid insight into his subject's interaction with others as well as his self-concept.

A second unit is the **hands, arms, shoulders, and chest**. They combine to form a functional unit to execute the commands of the brain or the impulses of the body. One can note size, shape, strength, degree of reaching out, degree of aggression, and conflictual signs within this functional unit. Does the subject draw his figures as reaching out for help? Are they reaching out in aggression? Are they fighting the world? Are they wresting all they can from others? Are they pushing away from others and the world to retreat within? Are they physically capable, or weak and inadequate? How does the physical strength of the figures contrast with the physical strength of the subject? These are but a few questions to be answered.

Thirdly, there is the torso or trunk of the body. The torso indicates strength features similar to those of the hands, arms, shoulders, and chest. Here clothing covers the body and is important symbolically as the facade or "front" which subjects present the world. Here is seen the **midline emphasis** of dependent persons, of those concerned with somatic difficulties. Physical impulses of the body may be open and emphasized, as in nudes or figures in bathing suits, or clothed rigidly, formally, as in Madison Avenue–Brooks Brothers attire. Indicators of control or restraint are ties, belts, jewelry which tend to cut off impulses symbolically associated with the torso.

Fourthly, there are the legs and feet. Here autonomy, self-movement, self-direction, and balance are indicated. One who draws long legs shows strivings for autonomy. A balanced or toppling figure shows emotional stability or instability respectively. Stability or instability may be revealed by symmetry or asymmetry. In male figures, feet are indicative of masculinity or doubts of masculinity; in female figures, legs indicate sexual concerns.

The interaction of the four major body areas is vital. Discrepancies in interpretation between different body parts must be resolved. At this point, Examiner considers the subject's background, family structure, chief complaint, descriptions of drawings, and spontaneous comments. It is helpful to contrast the subject's typical reactions to his problems and frustrations with the hypotheses gleaned from the figures he has drawn. Intricacies of interpretation become evident as one notes details, treatment of details, and meanings listed in the catalogue. Careful integration of hypotheses into a total personality picture is a **sine qua non**. Synthesis is the most difficult phase of examination and interpretation.

Final Report

The final report of DAP findings includes the following:

1. **Description of Testing Situation and Reaction of Subject to Testing.**
2. **Brief Description of Subject's Attitude to DAP.**
   Was he reluctant, eager, talkative, self-revealing? Quiet, methodical, impulsive? Did he seek reassurance, ask for further directions? Was he self-concerned, self-depreciating, rigid, contemptuous? Did he attempt to please Examiner? Was he inquisitive? How long did he take? Did he ask about the time, about type of drawing Examiner expected?
3. **General Impressions Conveyed by Figures Drawn.**
4. **Differential Treatment of Male and Female Figures.**
   Sex drawn first? More attractive sex? Sex closer subject's age? More capable sex? More active sex? Sex demonstrating the better mood? Differences in profiles, size, or placement. Sex subject identifies with. Sex subject spends most time with or details more and better. Sex with more conflict indications.
5. **Discussion of Interpretative Hypotheses Elicited from Catalogue.**
6. **Summary.**
   Discrepancies between interpretative hypotheses, clinical judgments, past history, present behaviors of the subject are resolved, as much as possible, into the final integrated personality picture developed.

A Few Words of Caution

No interpretation concerning human behavior should be made without full appreciation and use of the biosocial milieu of the subject. Interpretations conflicting with clinical impressions should be checked and carefully held in reserve until they are proved or disproved by strong validating evidence from the subject's history, or from further testing, or from present and future behaviors. Although the DAP provides considerable insight into personality structure and areas of physical concern, it cannot predict accurately the future since all circumstances which involve the subject cannot be predicted or controlled. If a clinician has reasonable assurances of events he can make shrewd guesses of future acts and outcomes. Such guesses, however, also can alter a clinician's behavior so that there is an increased or decreased probability for a subject to act out the Clinician's expectations. This is similar to a boy who is told he is a "bad boy." Coming to believe this, he operates on the basis of this belief with disastrous results.

On the basis of DAP research studies, it is not advisable to use the DAP to categorize individuals or predict future difficulties unless the clinical and historical data strongly substantiate the DAP findings. Even the most bizarre drawings indicate only present findings. Drawings may be almost devoid of the compensatory mechanisms used daily by a subject to function as a productive, socially acceptable member of a family or a community. Bizarre and radically different expressions of thought and feelings may be uncovered, but the controls over the apparent disabilities can be understood only by knowing the daily activities and past history of adjustment of a subject.

Clinicians who uncover apparent psychopathology should remember that their findings and conclusions, clear as they may seem, often are not acceptable to patients and therefore have limited effect. Forcing unacceptable insights or information on patients—even in a friendly manner and with the best of intentions—who are striving to keep such insights and materials hidden, courts disaster both for patient and Clinician. An important asset for effective clinical work is the ability to listen, gather data objectively, and suspend judgment. When it is necessary to make interpretations, one should be discrete, respectful and sincere, rather than spectacular in the presentation.

Clinicians know that all individuals have psychopathology, more or less, yet they function because they also have counter-balancing assets, compensatory behaviors, and idiosyncratic adjustment mechanisms. Thus it is of importance to consider strengths and modes of coping with weaknesses which maintain functional autonomy. Disdain of the weaknesses of others often indicates weakness in the disdainer.

The Draw-A-Person Catalogue

NOTES

A

ABNORMALITY indicated by: (also see WARNING INDICATORS)
1. **Bizarreness of figure.**
2. **Excessive incongruity of treatment of figure parts.**
3. **Over-symbolic figure treatment.**
4. **Silliness of figure treatment.**
5. **Internal organs showing through.**
6. **Extreme tension, shading, line pressure.**
7. **Confusion of profile with full view of head.** (Machover)

ACTION also see MOVEMENT
1. **Figure on display:** exhibitionistic, posing female, often drawn by adolescents with glamour aspirations.
2. **Active figure:** pre-adolescent boys. (Machover)
    . . . hyperactive individuals.
    . . . occasionally by quiet individuals with strong power strivings.
3. **Low activity level:** constricted rigid neurotics.
    . . . depressed individuals.
    . . . non-acute psychotics.
    . . . obese.
4. **Blocked movement:** schizophrenics.
    . . . highly anxious persons experiencing blocked impulses toward expression or sexual activities.
5. **Rigid body characteristics:** arthritics who feel physical strivings are blocked physiologically.
    . . . catatonics.
    . . . paranoids.
    . . . constricted neurotics such as obsessive-compulsives.
6. **Figures with firm stance reaching out to environment:** Normals dealing with world in stable, realistic manner.
7. **Differential treatment of action:** boys draw more active figures than girls, who are more concerned with display. Boys are expected to be powerful, successful, active in sports and business; girls are expected to be verbally quiet and socially active rather than physically striving. (Machover)

AGGRESSION
1. **Talon fingers:** hostility and aggression toward world.
2. **Figure with dark piercing eyes:** hostile awareness and suspiciousness of world, often found in paranoids.
3. **Figure with legs wide and arms up in gesture of challenge:** May indicate fighting to have own way and/or establish individualism.
4. **Flattened nose:** aggression; probably aggression was punished in youth and is no longer readily accessible.
5. **Emphasized nostrils:** unsophisticated primitive anger: literally "snorting with anger."
6. **Mittened, hidden, or cut-off hands:** repressive control of tendencies to act out hostile, aggressive feelings.
7. **Clenched hands:** clenched fist of angry man trying consciously to restrain anger.
8. **Heavily shaded hair:** deep aggression and anger.
    . . . may be indicative of a luxurious sexuality.

ALCOHOLIC IDENTIFIED by
1. **Orality:** is emphasized; ordinarily indicates oral dependency. (Machover) Also see DEPENDENCY, MIDLINES, POCKETS.
2. **Depressive features:** especially indicated by a lowered activity level.
3. **Dim facial features:** weak ego strength.
4. **Sexual conflict indicators:** Also see FEET, HAIR, NOSE.

NOTES

ANATOMY INDICATIONS

Discussion: These do not refer to nudes or outlined figures but to figures with anatomical features clearly indicated. Ordinarily these are pathognomic indicators but also occur in rare cases of subjects with unusual interest in anatomy combined with tension and hostility. In some cases there is malingering or a defiant teasing of the Examiner with attempts to reduce the examination to an absurdity so it will be less threatening.

1. **Anatomy indications:** repressed chronic schizophrenics.
   . . . occasionally actively manic individuals.
2. **Rib indications:** ordinarily are not considered pathological. (Machover)
   . . . probably indicates an emphasis on strength and beauty in male subjects.
3. **Sketchy lines at breast or pelvic girdle:** not considered to have anatomical indications.
   . . . shows rigidity.
   . . . may occur in involutional middle-aged women who are forced to re-appraise their sexual role and attractiveness for men.
   . . . may occur in adolescent girls concerned with the feminine role.
4. **Genitals in nude figure:** may be drawn by art students, due to training and/or interest.
   . . . persons in psychoanalysis, indicating current interest.
   . . . adolescents with sexual preoccupations and curiosity.
   . . . schizophrenics regressed to lower, less-controlled levels of emotional development.

ARTHRITICS identified by:
1. **Hard, outer shell:** indicating body impermeability.
   . . . may increase somatic concerns.

ARMS

Discussion: Typically arms are instrumental in: (a) "handling" the world, (b) rejecting others, (c) reaching out to others, (d) pushing away others, (e) drawing others near, (f) expressing anger, (g) defending one's self, (h) obtaining what one wants, (i) making love, (j) auto-eroticism. Arms indicate feelings and strivings for strength or weakness.

1. **Omitted:** may be a casual oversight. (Machover)
   . . . may indicate severe guilt feelings concerning hostility or sexuality. (Machover)
   . . . may indicate schizophrenic depression with active widthdrawal from people or objects: denial of the world and refusal to deal with it even symbolically. (Machover)
2. **Conflict treatment:** may occur when subject has ambivalent feelings concerning retreating from or dealing with the environment.
   . . . power strivings.
   . . . hostility and/or sexuality.
3. **Short:** lack of ambition. (Machover)
   . . . feeling weak and giving in to life. (Jolles)
4. **Thin:** feelings of weakness and futility. (Jolles) (Machover)
   . . . strong feeling of lack of achievement. (Machover)
5. **Winglike:** weak, schizoid contact with others. (Machover)
6. **Folded:** rejection of world. (Machover)
   . . . spurning of world and people because of suspiciousness and hostility. (Jolles)
   . . . rigid control over impulses to act out violently.
7. **Behind back:** guilt feelings and wish to hide hands.
   . . . need to control expression of aggression. (Jolles)
8. **Heavily shaded:** sometimes indicates sense of punishment. (Machover)
9. **Broad:** striving for strength is important; stresses physical power and brawn over brain. (Jolles)
10. **Bicep emphasis:** physical strivings.
    . . . may occur in male figures drawn by "masculine protest" female.
    . . . homosexuals.
    . . . adolescent males.

NOTES

11. **Long:** ambitious and striving for success. (Jolles)
    . . . demand for love and attention. (Machover)
12. **Overly-long:** ambition in compensation for feelings of inadequacy. (Jolles)
13. **Reaching into environment:** reaching for affection and social interaction. (Machover)
14. **Direction and fluency of arm lines:** indicate degree of extension into environment. (Machover)
15. **Broader at hand than at shoulder:** tends to indicate lack of self-control and/or tendencies to be impulsive. (Jolles)
16. **Outstretched arms:** subject needs emotional support when under stress.

B

BALANCE of subject indicated by:
1. **Balance of figure:** related to subject's feelings of mental balance
2. **Harmony, symmetry, proportion:** indicate extent of mental harmony or intrapsychic conflict.

BASELINE (See GROUNDLINE)

Discussion: Subject needs support. Therefore he draws baseline for figures to stand upon.

BEARD

Discussion: Even before the days of Samson and Delilah, hair and beard were symbolic of virility, strength, manhood. This interpretation continues to be made.
1. **Goatee:** a virility symbol indicating need to demonstrate masculinity in an unusual way.
    . . . may indicate artistic, anti-social, "beatnik," or schizoid elements.
    . . . if heavily shaded, over-concern with virility.
    . . . may occur in adolescents, homosexuals, old men, and some dull paranoids.
2. **Heavily shaded beard:** virility strivings and doubts about masculinity.
3. **Beard:** a phallic substitute: indicative of need to demonstrate virility. (Jolles)
    . . . status symbol.
    . . . power symbol.

BELLY

Discussion: The belly or gut is the center for taking in nourishment. Both food and children are carried in the belly.
1. **Distended:** tends to indicate feelings of physical weakness and somatic concerns of involutional or depressed males.
    . . . may indicate desire for role as child-bearer in women dissatisfied with present roles.
    . . . may indicate grasping, avaricious desire to take in as much as possible.
    . . . typical of children's drawings.
    . . . organicity.
2. **Empty or no stomach:** bizarre indicator may show schizophrenic emptiness, disintegration.

BELT also see WAISTLINE

Discussion: Traditionally the belt, since it separates the upper and lower halves of the body, has been a symbol of control. Physiologically the belt cuts off the upper or intellectually controlling part of the body from the lower or sexually expressing part of the body. The belt also provides a place for a purse, weapons, or other symbols of power and authority.
1. **Heavily shaded:** concern over control of sensuality.
2. **Absence of belt:** not unusual; fluidity, easy expression of emotions. Unless there are contrary indications, absence of a belt indicates flexibility and acceptance of sexuality.

BREASTS

Discussion: Traditionally the breast provides life-giving milk, symbolic of the mother and of receiving objects from the mother. The breast is associated with dependency, taking rather than giving.
1. **Heavy shading or disproportionate enlargement:** dependent, immature, self-seeking individuals. (Machover)

NOTES

2. **Large-busted, maternal female:** drawn by psychologically immature males and females reared in homes where they were dominated and overprotected by mothers or mother surrogates.
3. **Small:** may indicate stinginess in offering love, affection, approval to children;
   . . . if drawn by female, may indicate rejection of female sexuality.
   . . . may indicate feeling of rejection by mother. (Machover)
   . . . may indicate fear of mature female sexuality. (Machover)
4. **With low pendant line:** mother-dependent males who cannot sever "apron strings."
5. **Emphasis on breasts and pelvis:** by female, indicates strong identification with productive, dominant mother-image.
   . . . by male, indicates dependence on mother figure, and a strong seeking for love and approval.
6. **High and firm:** youthful female figure with youthful sex desires. (Machover)
   . . . may indicate young woman's rejection of more mature female sexuality for "boyish," "free love" equality with men.

BUTTOCKS
1. **Emphasized by shading, size, or erasures:** may indicate fixation at anal stage with resultant psychosexual immaturity. (Jolles)
   . . . possible homosexuality

BUTTONS
Discussion: Buttons have importance since they pose a barrier to the striving for independence in children. Considerable physiological maturation is needed for a child to develop the gross and fine motor controls necessary to button and unbutton clothing. Thus a child is forced to depend on the mother for this help long after gaining independence in areas of bladder and bowel control.
1. **Down midline:** may indicate continued dependence on mother or regression to oral dependency. (Jolles)
   . . . may indicate egocentric, somatic preoccupations. (Machover)
   . . . may indicate body consciousness with concern over submission and dependence upon authority. (Machover)
2. **Emphasis:** dependency, immaturity, and inadequacy. (Machover)
3. **On cuffs:** compulsive detailing with stereotyped, formal emphasis upon control.

C

CAP
1. **Cap:** may indicate immaturity.
   . . . may be an attempt to mask sexuality.

CHILDREN'S DRAWINGS are characterized by:
1. **Head:** is large (Machover)
2. **Hands:** are weak.
3. **Mouth:** appears chronologically early: emphasized to indicate oral dependency, needs for love, affection, and recognition. (Machover)
4. **Oral emphasis:** is normal in young children. (Machover)
5. **Wide upturned line for mouth:** desire to win approval from those child loves and needs. (Machover)
6. **Unseeing eyes:** are common; sign of dependence, shallow emotionality, lack of discrimination. (Machover)
7. **Transparencies:** are common.
8. **Spider-like figures:** expected through three to four years of age.
9. **Fingers:** usually non-existent or weak and two-dimensional; indicate inability to deal with environment.
10. **Clothing:** is non-existent or slight.
11. **Activity:** is common, indicates hyperactivity of young children.

NOTES

CHIN

Discussion: Traditionally the chin is associated with polar concepts of dominance and submission.
1. **Strong, projecting:** striving or need for dominance or ascendance, usually in social situations, not necessarily sexual relationships. (Jolles)
   . . . social aggression and leadership.
2. **Weak:** feelings of weakness, especially in social situations.
3. **Cleft:** striving and determination to work toward own goals.

CLOTHING

Discussion: Machover describes clothing as the compromise the subject makes between feelings of modesty and body display. The clothing on figures indicates surface levels of personality.
1. **Clothing drawn:** usually is crude, vague, or token representations. (Machover)
2. **Over-clothed:** clothes-narcissist. (Machover)
   . . . clothing used for social and sexual enticement. (Machover)
3. **Underclothed:** body-narcissist; self-absorbed, introverted, over concern with body development; tends to prefer fantasy to social intercourse. (Machover)
4. **Uncertainty whether to clothe or not:** may indicate subject is troubled by strong body-consciousness. (Machover)
5. **Jewelry:** combined with cosmetic features, hair emphasis, glamour indications, shows psychopathic adjustment in young female; this is a more valid hypothesis if sexual features of clothing are stressed. (Machover)

CLOWN indicates
1. **Trying to reduce testing to absurdity.**
2. **Attempting to reduce impulses and desires to harmless absurdity.**
3. **May have exhibitionistic trend.**
4. **May act the clown with others.**
5. **Above average intelligence and creativity.**

COLLAR
1. **High:** "stuck up," haughty attitude which stresses intellectual mastery of physical impulses.
2. **Stressed:** may indicate incoordination of body impulses and mental control with a resultant of subject seeking refuge in fantasy of self-esteem.
   . . . rigid control of physical impulses in one who cannot accept physiological needs, sexuality or hostility.

CONFLICT

Indicators	Most Frequent Areas	Hypotheses
1. **Shading**	Hands	Concern about adequacy
2. **Omissions**	Arms	Concern about adequacy
3. **Erasures**	Feet	Concern about autonomy and sexuality
4. **Lines**		
a. **Breaks in**	Nose	Concern about autonomy and sexuality
b. **Tremulous**	Crotch	Concern about sexuality
c. **Tremulous**	Legs	Concern about autonomy
d. **Jagged**	Neck-line	Concern about control
5. **Asymmetry**		
a.	Waist-line	Concern about control
b.	Ears	Concern about external dangers
c.	Eyes	Concern about external dangers

CONSISTENCY OF FIGURE TREATMENT
1. **Good:** shows relative equality of mood and behavior.
2. **Extreme:** may indicate flatness of affect and rigid conformity.
3. **Poor:** may indicate impulsivity, ego disintegration, mental deficiency, organicity.

NOTES

CROWN
1. **Crown:** is rarely drawn; a power symbol; may indicate grandiosity, strong needs for dominance, and a disruption in reality contact.

D

DEFORMITIES
1. **Deformities:** typically occur in areas of real deformity, present or past.
   . . . reveal real or symbolic difficulties with body area depicted as deformed.

DELINQUENTS characterized by:
1. **Soldiers or cowboys:** strivings for power and strength.
2. **Symbols of aggression:** guns, knives, clubs.
3. **Stress on size and strength:** increased head size indicates striving for intellectual control.

DEPENDENCE INDICATORS
1. **Midline emphasis:** especially buttons down midline or down axis of body.
2. **Concave, orally receptive mouth:** found in passive, receptive person who may become parasitic and demanding for attention, love, approval. (Machover)
3. **Large dominant female figure:** found in mother-dependent, over-protected males who feel weak and helpless because of dependence on strong females.
4. **Blind, unseeing eyes:** sign of dependence and shallow emotionality. (Machover)
5. **Weak hands and arms:** inability to cope with environment.
6. **Pocket emphasis:** dependent, receptive person.
7. **Infantile, youthful facial features:** rejects responsibility.

DEPRESSION INDICATORS
1. **Oral emphasis:** common. (Machover)
2. **Low activity level.**
3. **Bowed posture or seated figure.**
4. **Sour facial expression.**
5. **Lined forehead.**
6. **Disheveled hair.**
7. **Resistance to drawing body, feet, or legs:** lowered level of activity.
   . . . concern about autonomy.
   . . . nonacceptance of physical impulses.
   . . . lack of energy.
   . . . lack of enthusiasm. (Machover)
8. **Nose and foot conflict:** concern about sexuality.
9. **Unseeing eyes:** unable to face coping with world.
10. **Arms and hands omitted:** deep feelings of inadequacy.
11. **Body distended and misshaped:** feeling of physical disintegration.
12. **Poorly detailed.**
13. **Legs and feet drawn first.**
14. **Hair not shaded.**

DETAILING
Discussion: The figure drawn with more care and detail usually is the sex with the larger investment of libidinal energy by the subject.
1. **Excessive:** obsessive-compulsives who must structure a situation carefully so their repressed desires do not slip through their excessive controls.
2. **Complete lack:** severely disturbed and depressed persons give only barest outlines: figures convey empty, weak feelings as experienced by such individuals.

NOTES

3. **Few details:** common in children.
    - . . . mental defectives
    - . . . depressives
    - . . . organics
    - . . . evasive normals.
4. **Detailing Characteristics of personality types:**
    - . . . **compulsives:** minute details, erase often as they are overly-concerned with structuring every situation; they experience anxiety if things are not "just right."
    - . . . **paranoids:** excessively detail the eyes and ears; over-style the hair; are concerned with the supposedly hostile influences about them; are compulsively concerned with sexuality since to love means for them to drop their defenses against pain.
    - . . . **intelligent adults:** include more details of consistent, well-proportioned kind than **dull adults, children, depressives, neurotics, psychotics.**
    - . . . **mental defectives:** have poorly detailed drawings, reminiscent of children's drawings.
    - . . . **psychotics:** acutely disturbed may have bizarre details, anatomy indicators; chronic psychotics may be too controlled to draw more than stick figures or light outlines with gross distortion and lack of balance.
    - . . . **depressives:** weak, inactive, blind, empty figures.

DIAGRAMMATIC DRAWINGS show:
1. **Extreme symbolic thinking:** deteriorated schizophrenics. (Machover)
2. **Possible rigidity and constriction:** neurotic, regressed personalities, and rigid normals.

DIM LINES
1. **Regression to psychotic state:** may be indicated.
2. **Uncertainty and anxiety** of neurotic.
3. **Depression,** lack of enthusiasm and energy.
4. **Indicative of weakness** in area dimly drawn.
5. **Lack of assertiveness; shyness.**

E

EARS
Discussion: Ears are important as they pick up conversations and provide feed-back in relationships with other people. They provide sensory data for dealing with the external world and thus warn of dangers.
1. **Emphasis:** sensitivity to outside world.
    - . . . paranoids. (Jolles) (Machover)
    - . . . deaf persons. (Machover)
    - . . . auditory physical disability.
    - . . . occasionally in homosexuals who feel persecuted for their deviant sexuality. (Machover)
    - . . . neurotics extremely sensitive to criticism.
    - . . . extreme emphasis may indicate auditory hallucinations.
2. **Lack of emphasis:** refusal to listen to criticism. (Jolles)
    - . . . denial of concern over opinions of others.
    - . . . denial of auditory hallucinations.
    - . . . since inclusion of the ear is established at later age than other facial features, its omission is less significant than the omission of the more active body parts. (Machover)

EFFEMINATE SIGNS IN THE MALE FIGURE
Discussion: The signs below indicate femininity or identification with the female role in society. These signs appear in the drawings of overt homosexuals, homoerotic paranoids, obsessive-compulsives, at times, and in some normals who tend to be sensitive, idealistic, well-educated, or aesthetic in their interests.
1. **Long eyelashes.**
2. **Soft mouth with large lips.**
3. **Arched eyebrows.**

NOTES

4. **Precise coiffure.**
5. **Wasp waist-line.**
6. **Enlarged hips and buttocks.**
7. **High heels.**
8. **Glamourized facial features.**

EMPTY FIGURES tend to indicate
1. **Evasion.**
2. **Depression.**
3. **Mental deficiency.**
4. **Regression.**
5. **Schizophrenic feelings of emptiness.**

ERASURES

Discussion: Erasures indicate anxiety and overt dissatisfaction with the area drawn, the function of the area drawn, or the symbolic meaning of the area drawn. (Machover)
1. **More often** in neurotics.
    . . . obsessive-compulsives.
    . . . psychopaths with neurotic overlays. (Machover)
2. **Less often** in young children.
    . . . mental defectives.
    . . . regressed schizophrenics.
    . . . organics.
    . . . seniles.
    . . . manics.
    . . . depressives. (Machover)

EROTIC DETAILS
1. **Lack of:** inability to deal with sexuality growing out of the non-acceptance of sex in life; psychosexual immaturity or psychological evasion of sex.
2. **Excessive concern with:** sexual preoccupations in adolescents.
    . . . artists
    . . . persons in psychoanalysis.
    . . . sexuality inadequate or impotent.

EYEBROW

Discussion: The eyebrow, like hair, has sexual connotations.
1. **Trim:** social stereotype reflecting refinement and grooming.
    . . . women with glamour aspirations and body narcissism often critical of freely expressing their feelings. (Machover)
2. **Raised:** contemptuous, haughty attitude. (Machover)
    . . . questioning attitude.
3. **Bushy:** primitive, gruff, possibly uninhibited.

EYES

Discussion: The eyes are considered to be the "windows of the soul" and to reveal inner feelings. They also are the organs for making external contacts. Like the ears, the eyes provide sensory data to permit the ego to deal with the world, and are a cybernetic device for facilitating feed-backs.
1. **Disproportionately small:** desire to shut out world. (Jolles)
    . . . self-absorption. (Machover)
2. **Unseeing:** emotional immaturity and egocentricity.
    . . . childish or regressed adults.
    . . . low-grade mental defectives.
    . . . young children. (Machover)
    . . . dependence, shallow emotionality, lack of discrimination. (Machover)

NOTES

3. **Blind, closed, concealed by hat, or hollow sockets:** marked reluctance to view world.
   . . . possible hostility toward others.
   . . . tendency to avoid unpleasant situations. (Jolles)
   . . . tendency to exclude unpleasantness.
4. **Large, accentuated:** may be hostile and threatening.
   . . . may be glamourized individual, indicative of exhibitionistic trends, especially in girls.
   . . . male homosexuals. (Machover)
   . . . may be egotistical hysteric.
5. **Piercing:** paranoids over-alertness to world; suspiciousness of motives and behavior of others. (Machover)
   . . . limited breadth of vision but penetrating wariness in paranoid personality.
6. **Popeyed:** sexually excited. (Machover)
7. **Cockeyed:** confused thinking. (Machover)
8. **Large orbit with small eye:** strong visual curiosity with guilt, possible voyeuristic conflicts. (Machover)

F

FACE
Discussion: The face is the "front" presented to the world. It is the most reliable DAP indicator of mood; it sets the tone of the drawing by its expressions of love, hate, fear, aggression, meekness, inappropriate affect, rebellion, confusion, blandness or anxiety expressions.
1. **Strong emphasis:** concern about social relationships and outward appearance. (Jolles)
   . . . compensating for inadequacy, weakness, or lack of assertion by drawing an aggressive, socially dominant self-image. (Machover)
   . . . inner drive for social assertion. (Machover)
2. **Dim or omitted:** evasive about conflicts involving interpersonal relationships. (Machover)
   . . . withdrawal from social relationships.
   . . . timed. (Machover)
3. **Shape:** if oval, feminine, sensitive, aesthetic.
   . . . if square, powerful, masculine, power strivings.
4. **Drawn last:** has difficulty in social relationships.
   . . . desires to avoid self-revelation.
5. **Extra lines at naso-labial fold:** provides depth and maturity to face.
   . . . concern over emotional maturity or appearing mature. (Machover)
6. **Creased forehead:** intellectual aspirations or stress on emotional control.
   . . . chronic worrier; psychasthenic

FEET
Discussion: Feet provide the base for people or instruments of self-locomotion. Feet are a symbol of autonomy.
1. **Foot symbolism:** often a phallic symbol; important in drawings of adolescents and older males with sexual concerns.
   . . . may be too traumatic for adolescent girls to draw.
   . . . may be controlled by compulsive detailing.
2. **Symbolic meaning of feet:** feet provide index of the feeling of psychological or physiological motility.
3. **Omitted:** sense of lack of mobility or autonomy.
   . . . bed-ridden, depressed, discouraged. (Jolles)
4. **Very small:** constricted, rigid control of sexuality.
   . . . possible dependence on others. (Jolles)
5. **Very large:** tends to indicate excessive need for security.
   . . . strong need for firm foundation for support.
6. **Very long:** concern over male sexuality.
   . . . drive for independence. (Jolles) (Machover)
7. **Very pointed:** combined with talon fingers or other hostility indicators, supports hypothesis that repressed hostility or hostility feelings cannot be accepted.

NOTES

8. **Figure on tiptoe:** tenuous grasp on reality and strong need for flight from frustrating environment. (Jolles)
   . . . unusual ambition may be indicated.
9. **Over-detailed:** obsessive detailing.
10. **High heels:** homosexuals, homoerotics.
    . . . females with glamour aspirations.
11. **Feet pointing in opposite directions:** ambivalence, especially about strivings for independence. (Jolles)
12. **Clubbed foot:** immaturity and insecurity in footing. (Machover)
    . . . children, weak individuals.

FEMALE FIGURE
1. **Large, masculine:** masculine-protest female who envies male role.
   . . . women with limited heterosexual contacts.
2. **Small, weak:** grandiose males.
   . . . weak, sensitive, dainty females.

FINGERS also see HANDS
1. **Fingers:** tools for manipulating environment.
   . . . social contact points.
   . . . potential for aggression.
   . . . potential for communication.
2. **Large, spike-like or talon in form:** considerable hostility feelings. (Jolles)
   . . . paranoids.
   . . . overt aggression. (Machover)
3. **Clenched or cut-off:** strenuous efforts to suppress aggressive impulses.
4. **Stick:** infantile aggression. (Machover)
   See also **talon in form.**
5. **Petal or grape-like:** poor manual skill.
   . . . infantile emotionality.
6. **Heavily shaded:** guilt, probably concerning sexuality or hostility. (Machover)
7. **Clenched fist:** adolescent delinquents with rebelliousness near surface: figuratively shaking fist at world. (Machover)
8. **Mittened:** repression of aggression and possibly furtive outbursts of aggression.
9. **More than five fingers:** very ambitious, acquisitive. (Machover)
10. **Claw-like:** primitive aggression. (Machover)
11. **Very long:** regressed shallow adults.
12. **Excessive detailing of joints and nails:** trying to maintain rigid control of hostility.

FOREHEAD
1. **Emphasis on frontal bulge:** strong intellectualized goals and ambitions. (Machover)
2. **Reinforced:** not significant by itself except to show concern about mental control. Found in organics.
   . . . frontal lobe damaged, traumatic brain damage.
   . . . those with migraine headaches.
   . . . mental defectives.

FRONT VIEW
1. **Profile:** implications of exhibitionism, naivete, social communication.
   . . . more often in females and socially dependent persons.

G

GROUNDLINE (see BASELINE)
Discussion: A groundline possibly indicates feelings of insecurity or a need for a point of reference or a boundary. (Jolles)

NOTES

H

HAIR also see BEARD
1. **Heavily shaded:** excessive sexuality.
    . . . severe anxiety about sexuality or mental control.
    . . . anxiety over thinking or fantasy. (Jolles)
    . . . virility conflict with imminent possibility of moving into delinquent sexuality. (Machover)
2. **Long and unshaded:** ambivalence or hostility over sexuality. (Jolles)
3. **Disheveled or mussed up female hair:** in adolescents indicates impulsivity, often of sexual nature. (Machover)
    . . . male distrust of females: seen in alcoholics and paranoids with delusions centered on females.
4. **Messy female hair and precise male hair-do:** seen in psychosexually infantile males and indicates sexual disorderliness in connection with female and control with male. (Machover)
5. **Elaborate hair-do:** sociopathic females who enjoy self-display; vanity.
    . . . sociopathic or homosexual male who enjoys self-display.
    . . . adolescent girls with glamour aspirations.
6. **Prim, orderly:** in female figure indicates sexual control, possible barrenness. (Machover)
7. **Area covered by hair with degree of shading:** indicates extent and adequacy of virility and virility strivings. (Machover)
8. **Mussed:** associated with sexual immorality and lack of control. (Machover)
9. **Abundant in free arrangement:** associated with sexually attractive, active female. (Machover)
10. **Hair excitement:** relates to arousal of infantile sexual drives.
11. **Much attention to hair:** narcissistic, self-centered, vain.
12. **Hair unshaded:** depression, drop in libido.

HANDS also see FINGERS
1. **Large:** striving for strength; typical of adolescents or young boys, possibly compensating for weakness. (Machover)
    . . . tendency to make refined adjustments in social relationships because of feelings of inadequacy and impulsivity. (Jolles)
2. **Omitted:** feeling of inadequacy in dealing with environment. (Jolles)
    . . . guilt feelings about aggressiveness, hostility, sexual feelings. (Machover)
    . . . possible sense of castration weakness. (Jolles)
3. **Drawn last:** reluctance to deal with environment because of feelings of inadequacy or denial of power strivings. (Jolles)
4. **In pockets or behind back:** artistically sophisticated. (Cook and Wood)
    . . . evasion, unwillingness to deal with situation; psychopaths. (Machover)
5. **Heavily shaded:** guilt over a real or fantasied action: masturbation, assault, theft. (Jolles)
6. **Near genitals:** sexual preoccupations. (Jolles)
    . . . guilt over masturbation. (Machover)
    . . . defense against sexual approach. (Jolles)
7. **Disturbance of hand treatment:** common; possibly shows lack of confidence in achievements and social contacts. (Machover)

HAT also see CAP
1. **Hat:** conceals male sexuality.
    . . . male feelings of impotency.
    . . . unconscious male sexual compensation. (Machover)
    . . . female attempting to hide sexual impulsivity and present socially acceptable "good" facade.
2. **On a nude:** regressed, schizoid indication of infantile sexuality and compensatory fantasies of virility. (Machover)

NOTES

HEAD

Discussion: The head is the first part of the human figure children learn to draw. It is the most reliably drawn part of the body and expresses needs and responsiveness, intellectual strivings, and attempts to control the emotions. In the drawing of the head, the subject unconsciously portrays elements of intellectual concern: degree of preoccupation with fantasy, rational controls, concern with interpersonal relationships, and self-concept. It usually is the first part drawn and the last part to disintegrate in figures drawn by organically damaged subjects.

1. **Large:** shows strong intellectual strivings.
   - . . . considerable fantasy activity as source of satisfaction. (Jolles)
   - . . . organic concern over mentation. (Jolles) (Machover)
   - . . . children. (Machover)
   - . . . mental defectives.
   - . . . feelings of intellectual inadequacy with compensatory stress on intellectual achievement.
   - . . . possible grandiosity and egocentric attitudes based on feelings of inadequacy.
   - . . . aggression. (Levy)
   - . . . migraine headaches; brain surgery; indicates area of tension. (Machover
   - . . . youngsters with emotional and social maladjustments due to reading or school subject handicaps. (Machover)
   - . . . paranoid, narcissistic, intellectually righteous, vain persons: enlarged ego. (Machover)
2. **Small:** obsessive-compulsives. (Jolles) (Machover)
   - . . . obsessive-compulsive's expression of the desire to deny the site of painful thoughts and guilt feelings. (Machover)
   - . . . wish to deny the intellectual control which prevents the satisfaction of body impulses. (Machover)
   - . . . possible feelings of intellectual inadequacy.
3. **Over-detailed or over-emphasized:** suggests active fantasy. (Machover)
4. **Looking away from viewer:** possible sign of withdrawal. (Jolles)
   - . . . rejection of testing situation: evasion.
   - . . . rejection of environmental problems.
5. **Profile:** possible indication of evasion, slight withdrawal, guilt. (Jolles)

HEEL

1. **Emphasized:** psychosexually immature male. (Machover)
   - . . . possible homosexual trends, overt or unaccepted. (Jolles)

HIPS

1. **Emphasized:** possible homosexual tendencies.
   - . . . possible homosexual trends, overt or unaccepted. (Jolles)
   - . . . possible psychosexual infantility in male.
2. **Excessive shading:** homosexual panic, especially in paranoid individuals. (Machover)
3. **Confusion of hipline:** possible homosexual conflict.
   - . . . concern about female sexuality.

HOMOSEXUAL INDICATORS

Discussion: The following is clinically important: This list of homoerotic signs is indicative **only** of unconscious, covert, controlled homoerotic trends **or** aesthetic interests, sensitivity, dependency. To inform persons of unrecognized, unacceptable, covert homoerotic tendencies is anti-therapeutic and traumatic. Regardless of the degree or extent of the signs, such information must be used with great discretion and sound clinical judgment.

1. **Large eyes with long eye lashes in male figures:** (Machover) (Levy) (DeMartino) ...
2. **High heels in male figure:** (Machover) (DeMartino)
3. **Glamourized male profile:** (Levy)
4. **Soft mouth.**
5. **Arched eyebrows.**

NOTES

6. Precise hair-do.
7. Wasp waist-line in male figure.
8. Emphasis on male buttocks and rectum.
9. Poorly differentiates male and female.

HYSTERIC, IMPULSIVE INDICATORS
1. Irregular line pressure.
2. Lack of precision.
3. Jagged lines.
4. High variability.
5. Messy hair treatment.
6. Infantile facial features.
7. Weak hands and arms.

I

INADEQUACY FEELINGS INDICATORS
1. Very small figures.
2. Very large, weak, grandiose figures.
3. Weak hands and arms.
4. Blind or non-seeing eyes.
5. Club feet.
6. Petal fingers.
7. Thin, weak legs.
8. No feet.
9. Midline emphasis, especially buttons.
10. Pockets emphasized.
11. Large dominant female figure drawn by male.
12. **Introspective turning away from world:** shown by non-seeing eyes, being earless, looking away figures.

INCOMPLETE DRAWINGS may be due to:
1. Depression.
2. Evasion.
3. Low standards of achievement.
 . . . child; mental defective. (Machover)
4. Neurotic constriction.

J

JEWELRY see CLOTHING

JOINTS
1. **Emphasized:** obsessive-compulsive indicating concern with minute, unimportant details and excessive control of physical objects.
 . . . sense of faulty and uncertain body integrity.
 . . . arthritics.
 . . . somatic concerns of schizophrenics, body narcissists, obsessive-compulsives, arthritics. (Machover)

K

KNEES
1. **Emphasized:** homosexual tendencies. (Jolles)
2. **Joints detailed:** obsessive-compulsives.
 . . . somatic concerns.

NOTES

L

LEFT SIDE OF PAGE (also see PLACEMENT)

Discussion: The left side of page drawing is considered the **self** side, while the right side of page drawing is the **environment** side. (Machover)
   1. **Looking to left:** introspective, self-concern. (Machover)

LEGS also see FEET

Discussion: The legs function with the feet to provide support, balance, mobility, autonomy for the body.
   1. **No legs:** pathological feelings of constriction and dependence. (Jolles)
      . . . feeling of lack of autonomy.
      . . . castration feelings. (Jolles)
      . . . difficulty in accepting sexual desires.
   2. **Long:** striving for autonomy. (Jolles)
   3. **Large:** striving for autonomy.
      . . . ambivalence over strivings for autonomy. (Jolles)
   4. **Short:** feelings of immobility, lack of autonomy. (Jolles)
   5. **Broad stance:** defiance of authority. (Jolles)
      . . . denial of insecurity.
      . . . bracing for external shock.
      . . . stressing need for stability.
   6. **Crossed or tightly drawn together:** rigidity.
      . . . rejection of sexuality. (Jollies)
      . . . rejection of sexual approaches of others. (Jolles)
   7. **Atrophied legs:** feelings of weakness, inadequacy, growing sense of loss of power and autonomy due to physical degeneration in involutionals or seniles. (Machover)
   8. **Heavily shaded:** at times a sign of homosexual panic. (Machover)
      . . . may be indication of conflict concerning strivings for self-direction.
      . . . may be indicative of repressed concern with sexuality if drawn by female.
   9. **Legs and feet drawn first:** may be strong indicator of discouragement and depression.

LINE QUALITIES
   1. **Consistent:** adjustment may be considered to be stable.
   2. **Faint lines:** lack of assertiveness; possible tendency to be self-effacing and timid. (Machover)
      . . . anxious, timid, insecure: uses withdrawal as a primary defense.
      . . . uncertainty.
      . . . rigid control of impulses causing severe constriction and underproduction.
      . . . depression; lack of vitality; loss of enthusiasm.
      . . . ectoplasmic line indicates regression and withdrawal; typical of schizophrenics.
      . . . intellectual and introversive.
      . . . spiritual.
   3. **Heavy lines:** assertive, dominant, striving for power and control.
      . . . may indicate overtly hostile impulses.
      . . . may be sign of self-assurance.
      . . . may be indicative of anxiety if combined with shading and heavy pressure.
      . . . chronic, schizoid alcoholics and those suffering from fears of depersonalization. (Machover)
      . . . occasionally in excited schizophrenics or manics: sign of motor aggression. (Machover)
      . . . sign of tension and hostility. (Jolles)
      . . . organic brain damage.
   4. **Thick lines:** provide physical barrier to environment; typical of schizoid trends.
   5. **Variable pressure:** hysterics or cyclothymics: unstable, impulsive, easily frustrated. (Machover)
   6. **Jagged lines:** may be indicative of anxiety.
      . . . may show poor motor control.
      . . . may indicate low standards of equality.

NOTES

7. **Fuzzy, broken, and tremulous lines with light pressure:** schizoid alcoholics. (Machover)
8. **Heavy, smudged, profuse shading:** by children.
    . . . anxiety neurotics.
    . . . psychotics.
9. **Uninterrupted lines:** determination.
    . . . brain damage.
10. **Light, broken, uneven lines:** fearfulness, insecurity, inadequacy.
11. **Poor coordination:** overt tension, anxiety, possible brain damage (if lines are irregular).
12. **Sketching:** (abortive line movements or poor artistic sketching) anxiety, uncertainty, insecurity.

LIPS

1. **Full:** sensual, dependent, takes in rather than gives out in emotional relationships.
    . . . vanity, narcissism. (Machover)
    . . . in male figure drawn by male, effeminancy. (Machover)
    . . . sensitivity.
    . . . possible over-idealization.
2. **Cupid-bow:** exhibitionistic, sexually precocious, vain girls. (Machover)
3. **Erotic concentration:** oral eroticism. (Machover)
    . . . shading is done by more naive subjects.
    . . . cigarette or pipe indicates greater sophistication.

M

MALE-FEMALE FIGURES TREATMENT

Discussion: The differential treatment of the sexes is important, as it indicates areas of friction concerning sexual roles, hostilities, dependency, power strivings, and fixations at immature levels of sexuality.

1. **Infantile, sexually immature males:** may draw well-modulated, detailed, sympathetic male figures: ego-ideals.
    . . . obvious mother-figures with strength: one on whom such a male can depend.
2. **Homosexuals:** draw effeminate males and strong masculine females. (Machover)
    . . . sometimes glamourized males and females.
3. **Grandiose, exhibitionistic, egotistical males:** may draw weak female figures.
4. **Masculine-protest females:** tend to draw weak, inadequate males.
5. **Identifying with opposite sex:** these persons draw the opposite sex first, indicating sexual confusion as to roles.
    . . . may be unable to draw a figure of the same sex.
6. **Drawing opposite sex first:** indicates possible sexual inversion.
    . . . confusion of sexual identification and role.
    . . . strong attachment or dependence on opposite sex parent.
    . . . psychosexually immature: more likely to seek divorce, promiscuity, or excessive use of alcohol.

MIDLINE

1. **Emphasized:** strong dependency needs.
    . . . preoccupation with somatic symptoms. (Machover)
    . . . hysterical dependents.
    . . . possible feelings of body inferiority. (Machover)
    . . . emotional immaturity. (Machover)
2. **Emphasis with pressure:** suggests aggressive conversion of body conflicts. (Machover)
3. **Buttons down midline:** mother-dependence: looks to woman for strength and guidance; easily denies individuality to please a woman.
4. **Vague:** older persons concerned with their physical decline. (Machover)

MOOD OF FIGURE

Discussion: This category deals with the impressions formed from the figures. The adjectival list below may serve as an aid to describe drawn figures.

1. Happy, cheerful, joyful, buoyant, enthusiastic.

NOTES

2. Sad, unhappy, gloomy, depressed, despondent, discouraged, dreary.
3. Active, vigorous, animated, alert.
4. Apathetic, weak, passive, inert, cold, lethargic, dull.
5. Flexible, tractable, lithe, free, plastic.
6. Rigid, stiff, inflexible, unbending.
7. Stern, harsh, severe.
8. Appealing handsome, glamourous, angelic, debonair.
9. Forbidding, ugly, angry-looking, evil-looking, satanic, satyr-like.
10. Balanced, stable, strong, controlled.
11. Cock-eyed, off-balance, out-of-proportion, disproportioned, impulsive, erratic.
12. Warm, out-going, friendly, reaching-out, appealing, inviting.
13. Aloof, cold, self-contained, unfeeling, withdrawn.
14. Weak, infantile, adolescent, immature, boyish, childish.
15. Striving, determined, ambitious, aggressive, struggling.
16. Haughty, contemptuous, sarcastic, sardonic, supercilious, snobbish, looking-down-on-others.
17. Harsh, austere, authoritarian, dominant, demanding, strict, severe, disciplining.
18. Pompous, grandiose, self-centered, egocentric.
19. Blind, unseeing, self-concerned, introspective.
20. Bland, soft, mild, gentle, unoffending.
21. Empty, blank, vague, vacuous.
22. Benign, kindly, complacent, good-hearted, generous.
23. Puny, tiny, Lilliputian, insignificant, under-sized.
24. Gigantic, mammoth, colossal, dominating, towering, Herculean, stout, hardy, lusty, powerful, overwhelming.

MOUTH also see LIPS
1. **Emphasized:** oral eroticism.
    . . . strong dependency needs.
    . . . immaturity.
2. **Cupid-bow:** adolescent eroticism; youthful lust. (Machover)
    . . . narcissistic, vain adolescent girl.
3. **Exposed teeth:** strong sign of oral aggression of an infantile nature. (Machover)
    . . . tendency to act out hostilities orally: biting, cutting sarcasm.
4. **Wide, upturned:** forced congeniality.
    . . . tendency to present smiling, acceptable facade to mask less acceptable feelings.
5. **Slash of a mouth:** hostility and anger.
    . . . aggressive, over-critical, verbally sadistic. (Machover)
6. **Concave:** oral dependence. (Machover)
    . . . psychosexual immaturity.
    . . . demanding attention and approval.
7. **Rigidly closed:** refusal to reveal self.
    . . . rejection of dependent needs.
    . . . may be sign of suppression or hostility.
    . . . may be indication of guilt concerning fellatio.
8. **Sneering:** contempt for others.
    . . . aggression, hostility, probably because of feelings of weakness and insecurity.
9. **Emphasized:** food faddists.
    . . . alcoholics.
    . . . sexual difficulties relating to oral-genital contacts.
    . . . orally dependent.
    . . . gastric symptoms.
    . . . orally aggressive: uses profanity. (Machover)
10. **Tiny:** some rejection or denial of oral-dependent needs in rigid compulsives.
    . . . denial of oral-dependency in egostistical, independent persons.

NOTES

11. **Omitted:** severe rejection of need for affection.
    . . . severe rejection of orality. (Machover)
    . . . severe guilt feelings.
    . . . asthmatics. (Machover)
    . . . depressed.

MOVEMENT
1. **Activity:** tends to identify active persons willing to work through their problems.
2. **Hyperactivity:** compensating effort to control world and increase predictability.
3. **Passivity:** symptom of growing pathology in one with excessive feelings of weakness and inadequacy.

MUSCLES
1. **Emphasized:** may occur in art students.
    . . . male homosexuals.
    . . . self-absorbed.
    . . . self-centered body-narcissists. (Machover) (Jolles)
    . . . those with muscular atrophy.

MOUSTACHE
1. **Heavily shaded:** strivings for mature male sexuality.
    . . . occasionally a sign of hostility toward a male if drawn by a female.
2. **Small, neat:** controlled sexuality, self-concern, egotism.
    . . . occurs in drawings of some bright, controlled homosexuals.

N

NECK
Discussion: The neck joins the head and body; it provides an index of the coordination of mental control with physical impulses. (Machover)
1. **Long, thin:** lack of coordination of control of impulses, verging on schizoid pattern. (Machover)
    . . . may signify hostility, especially if accompanied by a reinforced collar.
2. **Broad, thick:** stubborn attitude, possible rigidity.
    . . . good assimilation of impulses. (Machover)
3. **One-dimensional:** infantile lack of control over impulses and desires.
4. **Omission of neck baseline in profile:** free flow of basic drives and impulses with inadequate controls. (Jolles)
5. **Emphasis by tie, necklace, or other cutting-off device:** stresses intellectual control over physical impulses. (Machover)

NORMALITY INDICATORS
Discussion: Nearly all "normal" individuals have areas of pathology. Most often, in psychological testing the Clinician or Diagnostician is forced to search for the pathological, and appears to under-value indications of strength and stability. Therefore, as a reminder, the author lists **some** characteristics of a "healthy" DAP performance.
1. **Size:** figures tend to be about six or seven inches tall; the female figure is slightly smaller or equal to the male, **but not larger.**
2. **Placement:** figures tend to be placed in middle of page, toward lower half.
3. **Starting Point:** most begin with head and facial features.
4. **Time:** most take 10 - 12 minutes or less for the DAP.
5. **Spontaneity:** figures show some animation, movement, i.e., are flexible, non-rigid.
6. **Proportion:** figures tend to be realistically-proportioned and lack distortion other than of a minor sort.
7. **Aesthetic Appearance:** figures tend to be symmetrical and pleasant to look at.
8. **Erasures:** minimal, but when occurring they improve the drawing.
9. **Line Quality:** lines tend to be consistent, showing steady pressure.

NOTES

10. **Sex:** self-sex usually drawn first; more time in detailing self-sex than opposite sex.
11. **Sexual Features:** sex of both figures obvious; female will have female breasts, longer hair than male, rounded hips. Male will have broader chest and shoulder, shorter hair than female, flatter hips, and more emphasis is placed on shading of male hair than female hair.
12. **Age Of Figures:** approximates age of subject.
13. **Belt On Male Figure:** sign of conventional controls.
14. **Formal Clothing:** indicates formal controls and tendency to being conservative.
15. **Eyes:** have pupils but not darkly accented.
16. **Nostrils Are Absent:** thus there is a lack of infantile aggression.
17. **Subjective:** accepts figures drawn without undue self-criticism.
    . . . does not demand reassurance or direction from Examiner.
    . . . mildly curious of what figures indicate about self.
18. **Sense Of Humor:** can accept drawing deficiencies with humor.
19. **Feet:** not emphasized.
20. **Ears:** not empahsized.
21. **Full Figure Drawn:** full figure drawn with only minor areas omitted.

NOSE

Discussion: The nose is a symbol both of sexuality and power strivings; probably more emphasis is placed on the nose as a symbol of power than of sexuality.

1. **Long:** aggression; ascendance-seeking.
   . . . socially out-going and active.
2. **Shaded:** possibly castration feelings in infantile male who projects defects to a female. (Machover)
3. **Button:** infantile sexuality.
   . . . childish dependency.
4. **Triangular:** power strivings.
   . . . infantile sexuality.
5. **Flattened:** power strivings which have been punished.
6. **Emphasized:** hints at phallic concern. (Machover)
   . . . adolescents and persons with castration fears. (Jolles)
7. **Sharp:** drive toward dominance with possible aggression.
8. **Hooked:** feeling that aging is effecting male sexuality.
   . . . sign of evil and avaricious thinking.

NOSTRILS

1. **Evident:** sign of primitive aggression; degree depends on size and shading: literally says "snorting with anger."
   . . . excessive control of anger except in close emotional relationships.

NUDES

Discussion: Nudes rarely are drawn, but are drawn by:

1. **Art students:** (Machover)
2. **Persons in orthodox psychonalysis.**
3. **Those preoccupied with sex.**
4. **Voyeurs.**
5. **Depressed schizophrenics.**
6. **Flippant, sexually preoccupied males.**

O

OBSESSIVE-COMPULSIVES tend to:

1. **Excessive detailing:** pockets, buttons, shoe laces, joints.
2. **Emphasize symmetry;** precision, balance.
3. **Excessive erasures.**
4. **Take much time to finish:** cannot leave drawings alone.

NOTES

5. **Draw virile bodies with long, powerful arms and tiny head:** desire to ignore rigid, painful mental control and submit to overt physical impulses. (Machover)
6. **Ask many questions:** try to force Examiner to structure test for them.

OMISSIONS

Discussion: The omission of a body part implies a conflict or concern in the omitted area. If the hand is the omitted or hidden area, see HAND. Before developing a conflict hypothesis, one should consider the immediate situation, social history, conflict status of area omitted, symbolic meanings of area omitted and other pertinent data.

ORGANICITY

1. Head out of proportion.
2. Head overly large.
3. Lines heavy and simple.
4. Synthesis weak.
5. No details, many omissions.
6. Figures overly large.
7. Sense of importance expressed by subject.
8. Rigidity of approach.
9. Stereotypy.
10. Heavy outlining of head.
11. Unusual pressure.
12. Framing of figure with additional lines.
13. Infrequent erasures.
14. Poor proportions.

P

PARANOIDS tend to:

1. **Emphasize head:** grandiose compensation for feelings of inadequacy.
2. **Emphasize eyes and ears:** over-concern with world; feelings that world is hostile and threatening.
3. **Draw profiles:** evasion and suspicion in testing situation.
4. **Draw piercing eyes: wariness of others:** "Watching out" for threats and dangers from others.
5. **Draw talon fingers:** extreme hostility and aggression directed at environment.
6. **Over-detail the hair:** great concern with sexual control.
7. **Have homoerotic signs:** sexual inversion in some paranoids.
8. **Refuse to draw.**

PELVIS

Discussion: The pelvis literally is the "cradle of civilization;" the seat of female sexuality; and man's most gratifying environment.

1. **Pelvic closure incomplete:** sexual conflict. (Jolles)
   . . . homosexual tendencies with possible guilt and anxiety.
2. **Large:** child-bearing fecundity. (Machover)
   . . . female superiority over male.
   . . . concern with child-bearing.
   . . . male dependence on mother or mother-image.
   . . . female concern with problems of child-bearing.

PERSEVERATION

Discussion: This refers to non-adaptive repetitions of a response. Perseveration often is manifested by dull or mentally deteriorated individuals, neurotics seeking refuge in safe, repetitive responses confined to a limited and secure area of activity, and malingerers.

NOTES

PERSON DRAWN

Discussion: Since drawings have many values for those who project their feelings toward people within the confines of a single drawing, subjects should be interrogated to obtain their concepts of the figures they have drawn. The Examiner tries to find if the figures drawn relate to concepts of self or others, whether drawings indicate existing or desired concepts of the world and people. Questions asked are open-ended, non-specific, and should not suggest answers.

1. **Ideal or facade:** the person the subject wishes to be or appear to be to others.
2. **Self-image:** as the subject sees himself.
3. **Authority figure:** one with whom the subject must deal.
4. **Significant person:** mother, father, sibling, or other significant person.
5. **Disliked person:** one toward whom the subject has ambivalent feelings: employer, spouse, neighbor.
6. **The opposite sex:** response to a sexual figure.
7. **Positive or negative person:** feelings toward men or women.
8. **Strong or weak person:** open confession of weakness and defects.
   . . . may indicate sincere effort to compensate for defects.
   . . . may be both confession and effort to change. (Machover)
9. **Mutilated person:** rejection of the concept symbolized by the mutilated body part. (Jolles)
   . . . severe mental upset.

PERSPECTIVE

Discussion: Perspective refers to the side of the drawn figure presented by the subject to the world.

1. **Profile:** more mature and sophisticated than front view which is relatively more naive and unsophisticated. (Machover)
2. **Disproportion of profile:** poor judgment. (Machover)
3. **Full view:** tendency toward exhibitionism and display in vain women, adolescent girls, socially outgoing males.
4. **Female full view, male profile:** by male is sign of self-protectiveness and readiness to expose female. (Machover)
5. **Confusion of head profile with full face:** rare, except in primitives, low grade mental defectives, organics, schizophrenics. (Machover)
6. **Head profile with full view body:** strained posture.
   . . . social uneasiness; guilt relative to social contacts.
   . . . drive to exhibit body. (Machover)
7. **Full figure in profile:** reluctance to face world.
   . . . tendency to hide self.
   . . . tendency to withdraw from world. (Jolles)
8. **Full figure and face without profile suggestion:** rigidity.
   . . . determination to face life directly. (Jolles)

PHALLIC SYMBOLS

1. **Guns, cigarettes, pipes, canes, shoes, noses.**
2. **Indicate:** fear of impotence.
   . . . hostility toward women.
   . . . psychosexual immaturity.
   . . . sexual preoccupation.
   . . . sexual strivings: Don Juan complex.

PHYSICAL DISABILITY OR ILLNESS

Discussion: Many psychologists and psychiatrists who use the DAP find physical disabilities and illnesses revealed in drawings by the conflict indicators or omissions in the affected areas.

PHYSICAL POWER

Discussion: Physical strength is emphasized by those who feel physically inadequate. One certain of himself in a specific physical area need not stress that area. (Machover) (Jolles)

NOTES

PLACEMENT

Discussion: Placement of figures roughly shows where the subject places himself relative to his environment on the drawing paper.

1. **High on page:** feels "up in the air;" no sound foundation.
2. **Above mid-point of page:** feels is working toward relatively unattainable goal. (Jolles) (Buck)
   . . . tendency to turn to fantasy for satisfaction of power striving (Buck)
   . . . may be aloof and inaccessible. (Buck)
   . . . might indicate optimism in working toward goals. (Machover)
   . . . may indicate haughtiness or "looking down" on others. (Levy)
3. **Center of page:** insecurity and rigidity.
   . . . need to maintain careful control. (Jolles)
   . . . normal degree of control and rigidity.
4. **Below mid-point of page:** feels insecure and inadequate with some depression. (Machover) (Jolles) (Buck)
   . . . concrete or "reality bound" in living and thinking. (Jolles) (Buck)
   . . . defeatist attitude; depression. (Levy)
   . . . need for solid foundation, balance, control.
   . . . may demonstrate stability, calm, balance. (Levy)
5. **Left side of page:** emotional dominance. (Jolles)
   . . . emphasis on past. (Jolles)
   . . . tendency toward impulsivity. (Jolles)
   . . . self-oriented. (Machover)
   . . . self-conscious. (Levy)
6. **Right side of page:** emotional control. (Jolles) (Buck)
   . . . making strong efforts to succeed.
   . . . environment oriented. (Machover)
   . . . extratensive.
7. **Upper left corner of page:** anxious; desire to shun new experiences and return to the past, or seek fantasy satisfactions. (Jolles)

POCKETS

1. **Emphasized:** infantile, dependent. (Machover)
   . . . affectional or maternal deprivation forms background for a psychopathic adjustment. (Machover)
   . . . adolescent with virility strivings which conflict with dependence on mother figure. (Machover)
   . . . oral-dependent: a taking, immature, non-giving person.
   . . . female who stresses independence.

PROFILE

1. **Controlled evasion:** or resistance to self-revelation.
   . . . may indicate mature control of feelings with refusal to be exhibitionistic.
2. **Full figure profile:** serious withdrawal and opposition tendencies. (Jolles)
   . . . controlled evasion or resistance to self-revelation. (Urban)
   . . . withdrawal tendencies not pathognomic unless additional signs of withdrawal are present. (Urban)
3. **Ambivalent profile:** one part of body facing different direction than another part of body.
   . . . tends to indicate extreme frustration with strong desire to abandon unsatisfactory situation. (Jolles)
   . . . introversive and extroversive trends, an ambivalence which produces confusion. (Urban)

NOTES

Q

QUESTIONS

Discussion: When a subject asks questions, he wishes the Examiner to structure the situation for him. Questions may indicate uncertainty as to the Examiner's expectations; they may show the typical uncertainty of the subject; or may indicate evasion of the situation, curiosity, anxiety, concern, confusion. All questions must be so answered that the testing situation remains unstructured. At the end of the testing, the Examiner may answer questions more fully or specifically, but with discretion and good clinical judgment.

R

RECTUM
1. **Emphasis:** a rare sign of paranoid or homoerotic trends. (Machover)

REGRESSION AND WITHDRAWAL INDICATORS
1. **Blind eyes.**
2. **Concave, receptive mouth.**
3. **Frozen movement:** figure is trapped in contemplation. (Machover)
4. **Profile looks to left.**
5. **Rigid profile.**
6. **Refusal to draw.**
7. **Weakness:** clubbed feet, weak legs, weak arms, petal fingers, diminutive figure.

RELUCTANCE TO DRAW

Discussion: Reluctance to draw may indicate:
1. **Timidity.**
2. **Anxiety.**
3. **Evasion:** fear of self-revelation because of feelings that all is not well.
4. **Depression.**
5. **Obstinance.**

RIGHT SIDE OF PAGE also see **PLACEMENT**

Discussion: The right side of the page is the **environment** side, while the left side is the **self** side. (Machover)

RUNNING FIGURE

Discussion: A running figure indicates a high level of energy directed primarily toward escaping from an unpleasant situation, according to Jolles. It also may be indicative of hysterical impulsivity.

SCHIZOPHRENIA INDICATORS
1. **Blocked movement:** has static, autistic, introversive features.
   . . . strivings toward achievement and power are fantasy-bound. (Machover)
2. **Left side of page drawing:** an introversive feature.
3. **Enlarged head:** active fantasy life.
4. **Ear and eye detailing:** in paranoid schizophrenics shows concern about auditory hallucinations and extreme suspiciousness.
5. **Rigid body:** constriction.
6. **Bizarre drawing:** loss of reality contact.
7. **Refusal to draw:** results from evasion or depression.
8. **Transparency:** internal organs showing; indicates anger and anxiety converted into somatic concern. (Machover)
9. **Confused succession:** usual succession is head to feet.
10. **Confused profile.**
11. **Gross disproportion.**
12. **Diagrammatic figure.**
13. **Formalized figure, indicative of compulsive fight for control.**
14. **Genitals displayed.**
15. **Dehumanization:** animal-like humans.

NOTES

SELF-CRITICISM

Discussion: Self-critical comments as "I can't draw.","This is terrible,", "Gee, does he look funny.", etc., indicate the following:
1. **Lowered self-esteem and possible depression.**
2. **Desire to avoid criticism by the Examiner.**
3. **Desire for reassurance from authority figures.**

SEQUENCE OF SEX

Discussion: Levy states that 87% of 5,000 subjects drew figures of their sex (same sex) first. In a sample of 16 homosexuals, 13 or 81% drew the opposite sex first. The following are possible interpretations of why the opposite sex is drawn first.
1. **Sexual inversion:** (Levy)
2. **Confused sexual identification.** (Jolles) (Machover)
3. **Strong attachment or dependence on opposite sex parent.** (Machover)
4. **Strong attachment or dependence on a member of the opposite sex.** (Levy)

SEXUAL CONFLICT
1. **Female legs heavily shaded.**
2. **Waist and neck constriction, shading, or emphasis.**
3. **Sexuality emphasized.**
4. **Lack of sexual differentiation between man and women:** male and female are drawn alike.
5. **Opposite sex drawn first.**
6. **Nude figures.**

SEXUAL DEVIANT

Discussion: Concentrating on a specific area or organ may result in erogenous emphasis. The extent of emphasis will depend on the strength of sexual desires and past experiences. (Machover)

SEXUAL SYMBOLS include:
1. **Hat.**
2. **Shoes.**
3. **Nose.**
4. **Pipe, gun, cane, cigarette, cigar.**
5. **Hair.**

SHADING indicates:
1. **Anxiety:** extent of anxiety is related to amount of shading.
2. **Free-floating anxiety:** extreme shading; may indicate self-doubt, self-criticism, or feeling unable to cope with a hostile environment.

SHOES
1. **Detailing:** in young pubescent girls is a sign of obsessive concern with sexual objects: abnormal curiosity and concern about male sexuality. (Machover)
2. **Pointed:** aggression.
3. **Heavily shaded:** sexual concern and striving.
4. **Lack of shoes:** primitive, unrepressed aggression and sexuality.
5. **Buckled:** exhibitionistic, narcissistic females decorate and elaborate shoes.

SHOULDERS

Discussion: Shoulders provide strength and power. With the hands, arms, and legs, the shoulders form a complex which indicates power strivings. According to Jolles, the left shoulder has feminine and the right shoulder masculine implications.
1. **Large:** feelings of strength; extreme concern for power. (Jolles)
   . . . adolescents. (Machover)
   . . . by female indicates masculine protest, strivings for strength and power over male. (Machover)

NOTES

2. **Small:** inferiority feelings. (Jolles)
   . . . de-emphasis of physical power with compensatory or substitute interests.
3. **Square:** with rigidity and hostility indicators points to extreme defensiveness and hostility. (Jolles)
4. **Well-proportioned and rounded:** a smooth, flexible, well-balanced expression of power. (Jolles)
5. **Lopsided:** emotional imbalance.
   . . . sign of a sexual role conflict.
6. **Erasures and reinforcements:** preoccupations with physical strivings and a drive for body development as an expression of power. (Machover)

SIZE OF DRAWING

Discussion: If the self-concept figure is **small**, the hypothesis is that the subject feels small or inadequate and responds to demands of the environment with feelings of inferiority. If the self-concept figure is **large**, the subject is responding to his environmental press with feelings of expansion and aggression. Any extreme indicates psychopathology. (Levy)

1. **Average:** about 7 inches.
2. **Size-space ratio:** may parallel dynamic relationship between the subject and his environment, or between the subject and his parental figures. (Levy)
   . . . may be related to subject's fantasy involvement.
   . . . may indicate degree of realistic self-esteem related to the expansiveness of the subject.
3. **Diminutive: or micrographic:** shrunken ego. (Machover)
   . . . feelings of inadequacy and concern in dealing with the environment. (Machover) (Jolles) (Levy)
   . . . regressed, vegetative schizophrenic; low energy level and weak diminutive ego. (Machover)
   . . . deeply depressed.
4. **Very large: or macrographic:** trying to prove self on paper.
   . . . grandiosity of paranoid with strong unacceptable, repressed feelings of inadequacy. (Machover)
   . . . fantasies of self-esteem.
   . . . may be characteristic of a manic who scatters his drawing over entire page or over-runs edges.
   . . . may show the high self-esteem of an aggressive psychopath. (Machover)
   . . . if poorly proportioned, empty, and meager may signify: mental deficiency, organicity, or the drawing of a child.
5. **Overruns Page:** lacks planning ability.
   . . . tends to be manic, overactive.

SMEARING

Discussion: By adults, smearing implies a regressive shading and severe anxiety. Smearing is not unusual in the drawings of children.

STANCE
1. **Feet wide apart:** assertive.
   . . . insecurity of footing is being compensated.
2. **Tight:** rigidity, restriction.
3. **Back to viewer:** rejection and defiance.
4. **Toppling:** precarious mental balance.
5. **Legs closely pressed together:** tense, self-conscious, awkward, resistive to sexual advances.

STICK FIGURES indicate:
1. **Evasion.**
2. **Rigidity:** intellectually guarded.
3. **Psychopathy:** made by those who find interpersonal relationships distasteful. (Jolles)
4. **Insecurity:** self-doubting. (Levy)

NOTES

STOMACH also see BELLY

Discussion: The stomach is that part of the body most susceptible to anxiety and its conversion into physical complaints: note the high incidence of gastrointestinal conditions of psychogenic origins. Psychodynamically, a full stomach is associated with feelings of well-being, while an empty stomach is associated with feelings of loneliness and emptiness. Typically, schizophrenics feel hollow and empty as do most depressed and emotionally deprived persons. Their drawings may reveal this.

STROKING
1. **Long:** control. (Jolles)
2. **Short:** impulsivity. (Jolles)
3. **Jagged:** hostility.
   . . . possible impulsivity. (Jolles)
4. **Sketchy:** insecurity and anxiety.
   . . . sign of feeling of inadequacy if pressure is light.
5. **Toward body:** introversion. (Levy)
6. **Away from body:** extroversion. (Levy)
7. **Pressure:** indicates energy level. (Levy)
8. **Heavy pressure:** indicates anxiety and tension.
9. **Vertical pressure:** indicates determination, assertion, masculinity.

SUCCESSION

Discussion: Most subjects begin with the head and work down toward the feet.
1. **Hesitation to go below head or waist-line:** reluctance to face conflicts relating to the symbolic meanings of areas avoided. (Machover)
2. **Confused:** impulsive, manic, and overactive.
   . . . confused schizophrenic.
3. **Bilateral development of tiny areas:** rigid, compulsive. (Machover)
4. **Facial features drawn last:** maladjustment involving reluctance or inability to face emotional commitments. (Machover)
   . . . schizoid trends.

SURGICAL CASES

Discussion: Meyer, Brown, and Levine studied drawings made by patients before and after surgery. Surgeries involved breast removals, leg amputations, and eye and ear surgery. All surgical areas were indicated in DAP drawings as areas of anxiety. Regressive features of figures tended to clear up or diminish after surgery, indicating that efforts were being made to compensate and accept the results of the surgery.

SYMMETRY
1. **Bilateral:** rigidity and repression. (Machover)
   . . . bizarre effects may indicate paranoid schizophrenia. (Machover)
2. **Extreme:** compulsive, emotionally cold and distant. (Machover)
3. **Marked disturbance:** neurotics with feelings of physical awkwardness and inadequacy.
   . . . hypomanic or hysteric with impulse disturbance. (Machover)
   . . . childishness of hysteric.
   . . . severe anxiety neurotic.

T

TEETH

Discussion: An emphasis placed on teeth indicates oral aggression, biting sarcasm, a sardonic view of life, superciliousness or other weaknesses which must be compensated. (Machover)

THEME

Discussion: Figures drawn often tell stories and present a variety of themes.
1. **Cowboy:** aggression in fantasy life directed toward active, physical expression of feelings: children and delinquent adolescents.
2. **Snowman:** evasion of body problems.

NOTES

3. **Clown, cartoon, silly figures:** may be expressing self-contempt or self-hostility.
   . . . reducing examination or Examiner to an absurdity.
4. **Older person:** striving for maturity and control.
5. **Younger person:** use of childish defenses.
   . . . longs for freedom of expression and limited responsibilities of childhood.
   . . . emotionally immature.

THUMB
1. **Rigid:** concerned with masturbation. (Machover)

TIE
1. **A phallic symbol:** concern with male sexuality.
   . . . control of sexuality and physical impulses.
2. **In motion:** occasionally indicates overt sexual aggression.
   . . . intense sexual preoccupation. (Machover)
3. **Bow-tie:** informal, youthful, sexually promiscuous.

TOES: (EMPHASIZED)
1. **Primitive aggression.** (Machover)
2. **Confined:** confinement of aggression. (Machover)

TOPPLING PERSON
1. **Sense of imbalance:** pre-schizophrenic. (Hammer)
   . . . personality in state of flux, unstable.

TOPS PAGE
Discussion: One who tops the page or over-draws the bounds of the page tends to over-extend himself in relationships with others and to have an extremely active fantasy life. Cyclothymic personality.

TRANSPARENCY: (of figures)
1. **Voyeuristic trends.** (Machover)
   . . . break in judgment. (Machover)

TRUNK
Discussion: The trunk of the body is the origin of physical impulses.
1. **Omitted:** rejection of physical impulses.
   . . . involutional males.
   . . . children. (Machover)
   . . . loss of body image. (Jolles)
2. **Long and narrow:** schizoid characteristic. (Jolles)
3. **Failure to close:** sexual preoccupation. (Machover)
4. **Very small:** denial of body drives. (Jolles)
   . . . feelings of inferiority and physical weakness. (Machover)
5. **Very large:** many unsatisfied instinctual drives. (Jolles)
   . . . strivings for physical dominance. (Machover)
6. **Trunk of opposite sex heavily shaded:** hostility toward opposite sex. (Machover)

NOTES

W

WAIST-LINE also see BELT

Discussion: The waist-line cuts across the origin of the physical impulses. Machover notes: above the waist-line are areas of physical strength in the male, while below are sexual areas. In the female, above are the breasts with their life-giving fluids, and below are sexual and reproductive areas.

1. **Emphasized:** sexual control.
2. **Heavily shaded or cut-off:** extreme control of sexuality perhaps because of guilt feelings or sense of impending loss of sexual controls.
   . . . combined with neck conflict, rigid stance, lack of movement, cutting off or hiding of hands, and rigidity of arms, would indicate excessive rigidity and brittleness of control with failure to deal with demands of the world.
3. **Refusal to draw below waist-line:** sexually disturbed and blocked. (Machover)
4. **Delay in drawing:** a block in dealing with the body area of sexuality.
5. **Extremely tight:** suggests precarious control which results in temperamental outbursts. (Machover)
   . . . narcissistic, self-centered, vain.

WARNING INDICATORS OF SEVERE MENTAL DISTURBANCE (Also see SCHIZOPHRENIA)

1. **Sightless eyes.**
2. **Anatomy indicators.**
3. **Gaping mouths.**
4. **Leering mouths.**
5. **Clutching fists.**
6. **Bestial qualities.**
7. **Extreme, smudged shading.**
8. **Slashed mouths.**
9. **Talon fingers.**
10. **Omission of important parts:** as arms, hands, legs.
11. **Rigid, diagrammatic figures.**
12. **Lack of balance, toppling over.**
13. **Nudes with genitals emphasized.**
14. **Scribbling.**
15. **Confusion of profiles in the face.**
16. **Tiny, empty drawings.**
17. **Large, grandiose drawings which overrun the page.**
18. **Crossed eyes.**

End

NOTES

NOTES

NOTES

NOTES

NOTES

NOTES

NOTES

NOTES

NOTES

NOTES

NOTES